I am your pet

Best friends' care guides

Hamster

Written by
Matthew Rayner BVetMed MRCVS

Photographed by
Frank Greenaway

PANGOLIN

Editorial Director: Louise Pritchard
Design Director: Jill Plank
Editor: Annabel Blackledge
Art Editor: Kate Mullins

Pangolin Books would like to thank Sarah and Peter Charmley
of the Minx Hamstery for their help.

First published in Great Britain in 2004
by Pangolin Books
Unit 17, Piccadilly Mill, Lower Street,
Stroud, Gloucestershire, GL5 2HT

Reprinted 2005

A CIP catalogue record for this book is
available from the British Library.

ISBN 1-84493-003-3

Colour reproduction by
Black Cat Graphics Ltd, Bristol, UK
Printed in China by Compass Press Ltd

AB		MO	
MA	12/05	MR	
MB		MT	
MC		MW	
MD			
ME			
MG			
MH			
MM			
MN			

Ooooh,
is this book all
about me?

Contents

4   This is me

6   All shapes and sizes

8   Wild life

10 Be prepared

12 The right choice

14 Feeding time

16 Housework

18 Body talk

20 Making friends

22 Fun and games

24 Keeping me healthy

26 Good company

28 Having babies

30 Glossary

31 Find out more

32 Index

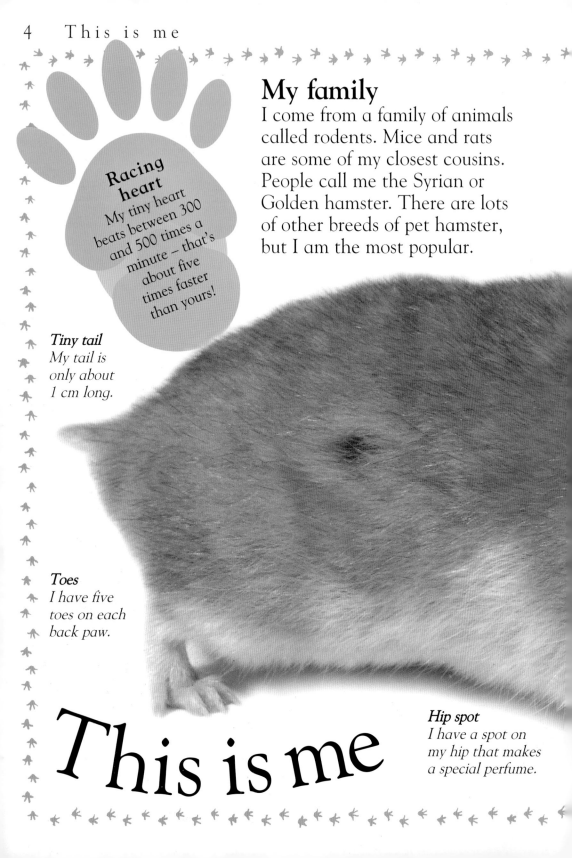

Racing heart
My tiny heart beats between 300 and 500 times a minute – that's about five times faster than yours!

My family
I come from a family of animals called rodents. Mice and rats are some of my closest cousins. People call me the Syrian or Golden hamster. There are lots of other breeds of pet hamster, but I am the most popular.

Tiny tail
My tail is only about 1 cm long.

Toes
I have five toes on each back paw.

Hip spot
I have a spot on my hip that makes a special perfume.

This is me

A little help

You will need an adult to help you take care of me. He or she will make sure that we are both safe and well, and that we do not hurt each other by mistake. You can teach your adult helper everything you learn from this book.

Hamster sense
My eyesight is bad, but I can hear and smell better than you can.

I just can't help being so cute!

Teeth
I may look cute, but my mouth is full of strong, sharp teeth!

Fingers
I have four fingers on each front paw.

Fat face
Don't worry if my face looks fat and lumpy. I have pouches in my cheeks that I use to hold food and bedding.

All shapes

Furry friends

My hamster friends come in all shapes and sizes. There are tiny dwarf hamsters, Russian hamsters, Chinese hamsters, hairy hamsters, spotted hamsters – and even hamsters that change colour!

I think I am in pretty good shape!

Golden hamster

You will probably see lots of hamsters like me in pet shops. Most Syrians have beautiful golden coats like mine. I make a good pet because I don't often bite and I like to be picked up.

Dwarf hamsters

Dwarf hamsters are my smallest friends,
and they come in all sorts of colours.
All dwarf hamsters are related to
Dwarf Russian hamsters.

and sizes

Campbell's Dwarf
This little
hamster has
hairy feet.

Winter Whites
These dwarf
hamsters' coats
sometimes turn
pure white in
the winter.

Perfect pets
All hamsters like to
eat, sleep and play, and
we all make good pets.
Dwarfs can be hard
to catch, so
Syrians suit new
owners best.

Dove
This Syrian is a
rare dove colour.
She stands out
from the crowd!

Chocolate tort
This Syrian is
called a chocolate tort. He is brown
with a white band around his belly.

A coat for all occasions

Long coats, short coats, smooth coats
– we hamsters have it all. Some types
of coat are rare, but if you search
hard you will find your perfect pet.

Teddy bear
This fluffy Syrian is
known as a 'teddy
bear' hamster.

Wild life

Eating and sleeping

My wild hamster relatives live in the desert and spend most of their time searching for food. They look for food at night, when it is not too hot. They sleep during the day.

Taste of freedom

Like my wild cousins, I love searching and sniffing for food. If you hide things like nuts and seeds around my cage, I will hunt happily for hours.

Large litters

Wild female hamsters usually have eight babies. But they can have as many as 25!

Staying together

Wild Syrian hamsters stay with their family until they are five or six weeks old. Then they go off on their own.

Finding food

Wild hamsters use their good sense of smell to find food.

Wild at heart

Like wild hamsters, I am sleepy in the day, awake at night and happiest when I am busy. I am pretty good at looking after myself too.

Keeping clean

I lick my paws then rub them on my fur to keep it clean.

Mmmm, I can smell breakfast.

The basics

Before you buy me and take me home, you must get everything I need. A cage, bedding, some food and a water bottle are most important. You can always get the extras later.

Safe house

If you have a cat, a cage with solid sides is best. Cages like this also suit my dwarf friends, who can slip between the bars of other cages.

Escape artist
I am extremely good at escaping. I can squeeze through tiny spaces and even pile up my bedding so that I can reach the top of my cage.

Be prepared

House hunting

Hamster cages come in all shapes and sizes. Buy me a home that is easy to clean, secure, roomy and airy. Then I will be safe and comfortable.

Tunnels and tubes

I love crawling through tunnels. It's a bit like being a wild hamster burrowing in the sand.

Ahhh, that was a lovely long sleep.

Natural plant fibre

Which bedding?
I like my cage to be lined with a thick layer of plain wood shavings. And I need a cosy pile of soft shredded paper, hay or plant fibre bedding inside my nest box.

Shredded paper

Wood shavings

Coloured plant fibre

Nest box
I need somewhere dark and warm in my cage where I can sleep and store my food. A box like this is perfect.

Bedtime
If I wake up during the day I can get grumpy. Put my cage in a quiet place and give me a box in which to hide.

Food and water
I need food and fresh water at all times. A water bottle fixed to my cage is best, so I cannot spill it.

A little air
I don't like draughts, but I need fresh air. A cage with a mixture of solid sides and narrow bars suits me best.

The right

The right time
The best time to go to choose a hamster is late afternoon. Hamsters will be sleepy earlier in the day and might not feel like saying hello to you.

Mmmm, I could lie here all day.

It's a boy!
I am a male hamster. I look quite like my sisters, but my body is rounder with a bulge at the back end. The two openings I use to go to the toilet are 1 or 2 cm apart.

Finding your hamster

You can buy your hamster from a breeder. Look at notices in pet shops and in newspapers for hamsters for sale. If you cannot find any, you can buy your hamster from a good pet shop.

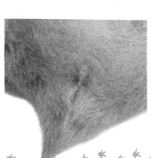

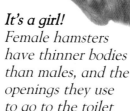

It's a girl!
Female hamsters have thinner bodies than males, and the openings they use to go to the toilet are closer together.

choice

Please take me home with you ...

LOOK OUT!
* **Be very careful** when you buy your hamster. If his cage is dirty or the hamsters look ill or are very young, do not buy one. Try somewhere else.

Pick me!
I have bright, clear eyes, a clean bottom, clean mouth and clean nose. I am also nice and plump. Make sure the hamster you choose looks as healthy as I do.

Nice-natured
Hamsters like me make perfect pets. I am friendly and not too shy.

Eating habits

Like a wild hamster, I am happy to try all sorts of different foods. You don't have to feed me at the same time every day, but please make sure there is always some food in my cage. My favourite time to eat is at night, when you are fast asleep in bed.

Feeding time

Peanuts

Pellets

Flaked maize

Locust bean chips

Flaked peas

Secret snacks
I like to collect food in my pouches. When they are full, I empty them in a quiet corner. Then I can have a little nibble when no one is watching.

A little variety
I like to eat a good mixture of different seeds and grains. The variety helps me to stay interested in my food.

Wheat

Sunflower seeds

In the mix
You can buy hamster mix in pet shops. It should include things like wheat, maize, sunflower seeds, peanuts and special hamster pellets.

Yum, I think I'll save this for later.

Tasty treats
Hamsters can eat some human foods such as breakfast cereal, natural yoghurt and toast. Give us only a tiny bit at a time though.

LOOK OUT!
* **Don't feed** me raw potatoes, buttercups, onions or citrus fruits because they will make me very unwell.
* **Never feed** me chocolate, crisps or sweets. No matter how nice they taste, they could make me ill.

Fruit and veg
We love things like bananas, apples, cucumber, raw peas, carrots and green beans. We also like to eat a bit of fresh hay and grass. You can give us a small piece of fresh food every day.

Water water!
I don't usually drink much water each day, but you should still fill my bottle with fresh water. Keep an eye on how much I am drinking. If I suddenly start to drink a lot, it could be a sign that I am not very well.

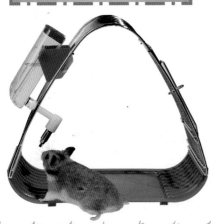

Housework

Safe place
*Put me in a
safe place while
you clean
my cage.*

I am
coming back.
Are you ready?

Clean routine

You must keep my cage nice and clean so that it
doesn't start to smell or attract germs. Take out any
uneaten fresh food every day because it will go bad.

Washing up

Wash my cage and nest box properly at least once a week. Use washing-up liquid. Never use bleach. Rinse and dry the cage carefully.

Making my bed

When you change my nesting material, please leave it outside my box. I like to make my own bed. I drag the bedding into my box and burrow in it to fluff it up.

Out with the old

Throw away the wood shavings from the floor of my cage. Save a bit of nesting material so that the cage still smells of me.

In with the new

Wash and dry my cage and nest box, then replace the wood shavings. Last of all, give me a pile of new nesting material.

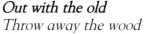

LOOK OUT!

* **Don't leave** me with wet bedding. Replace it as soon as you notice it.
* **On cleaning** day, throw away all old food in my cage. Mouldy food might make me ill.

Back where I belong

When you put me back in my cage, leave me alone for a few hours. I like time to settle in again.

Many moods

Like you, I have different moods and my own funny little ways. Sometimes I feel grumpy or shy and sometimes I feel like being naughty. You can often guess my mood from the way I behave and move.

Body talk

Curious creature

When I am curious, I open my eyes wide and move around a lot. I sniff things in my path and investigate everywhere. I act like this only when I am happy and relaxed.

Taste test
If I am feeling really curious, I might investigate things with my teeth.

Flight or fight?
If I am angry or scared, I will usually try to run away. If I cannot escape, I may curl up in a ball or roll away from the scary thing. If I am feeling really brave, I may try to fight or bite.

Tired and grumpy
I can get very cross when I am woken up at the wrong time. If my ears are flat and my eyes are half closed, this is a sign to leave me alone.

Under investigation
I might decide to investigate you. My feet and nose will tickle a bit!

LOOK OUT!
* **Don't pick me** up just after you have eaten. My sense of smell is good but my eyesight is not, and I may mistake your finger for some food. I am not being naughty. I am just confused.

Busy body
When I feel like it, I can move very fast indeed. I can squeeze into places much smaller than you'd think.

Scent spreading
When I am out of my cage I may go to the toilet a lot. I don't mean to be messy. I am spreading my scent around.

Mischievous – what, me?

Feeling silly
I can be quite mischievous when I am in the mood. I might kick my bedding out of my cage. Or I might show off by getting into funny places and positions.

Hold me close

Once I am used to you feeding and
stroking me, you can try to pick
me up. Scoop me up gently and
cup me in both hands.
Don't squeeze me too
hard or lift me up high.

> Don't hug
> me too hard. I am
> only little!

Wriggly worm
*I can be a bit
wriggly, so be
careful not to
drop me.*

Try again later
*If I am very wriggly, it
may mean I am scared. Put me
back in my cage and try again later.*

Making friends

Hand feeding

You can gain my trust by letting me eat food from your hands. I will soon get used to your hands if you put them in my cage and let me investigate them in my own time.

Tempting treats
When I am really tame, you can feed me while you are holding me.

I wonder what games we'll play tomorrow.

Toothy tip
I bite only if I am scared. All I need is a little bit of time to get used to you. If you are worried about my teeth, try wearing gloves to handle me at first.

Faithful friend

Soon I will learn when to expect you to come to see me. I might even be waiting for you when you come to feed or play with me. You are my best friend after all!

Fun and

Going nowhere fast

Even if you play with me every evening, I will still spend a lot of time in my cage. Give me an exercise wheel so that I can go for a run whenever I feel like it. Then I will not get too fat.

Safety first
My wheel must be solid so my legs don't get caught.

Playing out
You can let me out to run free every now and then, but be careful where you walk! Keep a close eye on me. I can move fast, squeeze into tiny places and get stuck out of reach.

Busy is best

My wild cousins travel up to
8 kilometres a night looking for food.
If I am left in my cage all the time
with nothing to do, I might get
bored. I will probably
do my very best
to escape.

games

You know, I think I might ...

*Next stop,
the kitchen!*

... have come this way before!

Up, up
and away
*I am very
good at climbing.
I love cages with more
than one level, and I
can even climb up
vertical tubes and
curtains. The only
problem is that I am
not so good at getting
down again afterwards!*

Room to roam
*I love cages that are made
up of rooms joined by tunnels.
By the time I've explored
everywhere, I've forgotten
where I started from!*

Keeping

Health matters

Check me over every evening to make sure I am in tip-top condition. Make sure I am my usual self. Check that I am not scratching and have not lost any fur. I should have a clean bottom and clear, bright eyes.

Paws and claws

Check my feet every evening. If I get lots of exercise, my claws should not get too long. As I grow older and less active, I may need to visit a vet to get my claws clipped.

Acting funny

If I seem quieter or grumpier than usual, it might mean I am ill or injured. Keep a close eye on me, and if I don't get well quickly, take me to a vet.

me healthy

The brush off
Brush me gently with an old toothbrush. This is a good time to check that my skin and fur are healthy. It feels nice too!

Something to nibble
Hamsters' teeth never stop growing. We need to chew things to stop our teeth getting too long. Fruit-tree twigs make ideal chewing sticks.

Oooh, stop! That really tickles!

Ask the vet
If you are worried about me, take me to see a vet, especially if I have an upset tummy or stop eating or drinking. The vet might give me some medicine, and will tell you how to look after me until I am feeling better.

Ear, ear
Gently fold back my ear flaps and look into my ears to make sure they are clean and not sore.

Good company

Group hug
My Dwarf Russian friends like to cuddle up.

Fighting talk
Even in the wild, Syrian hamsters like me eat and sleep alone. Never introduce me to another hamster because you'll end up with a furry fight on your hands.

Close companions
Dwarf hamsters can live together if they meet at a young age. Don't mix boys and girls because you'll have a whole family of hamsters to care for!

Solitary Syrian
I don't like living with other hamsters, so I need you to be my best friend. I will depend on you for everything.

LOOK OUT!

* **Never leave me** alone for more than 24 hours. I will need fresh water and food, exercise and someone to play with. If you go on holiday, you will need to arrange for someone to look after me.

Friends for life
A puppy will get used to me more quickly than an older dog will.

You're a funny looking puppy!

Not my friends

I do not get on well with rats, gerbils and mice. We may fight. Cats are not friends of mine either. They might decide to eat me!

Little and large
I will probably get on with a dog best, but never leave us alone together. Even a friendly dog could hurt me by mistake because I am so small.

Do you want to share my tea?

Having babies

New arrivals

When hamsters are four to six months old, they can have babies, or pups. The female is pregnant for about 16 days, and then she gives birth to the babies – usually between eight and ten of them. The female looks after the babies and feeds them with milk from her body.

Early days
This is one of my friends at three days old. She was blind, deaf and hairless, and needed to stay close to her mum.

On the move
After 12 days, she could hear and had grown some soft fur. She was still blind, but had begun to move about more.

Mum's the word
When a hamster is expecting babies, her belly swells up and she eats more food. She builds a nest for her babies. She needs lots of peace and quiet.

Bigger and braver
At 16 days, the young hamster had a full coat and could see. She was big enough to explore.

Leaving mum
At three weeks, she left her mum and lived with her sisters. Her brothers lived in a separate cage.

My own space

Hamsters are ready to leave their family when they are six weeks old. I didn't miss my family when I left it because I like to have my own space.

LOOK OUT!

* **Don't let your** hamster have babies unless you are sure you can find good homes for them. There are already plenty of hamsters looking for homes. You will need to learn a lot about hamsters before you are ready to help your hamster look after her babies.

Glossary

bedding
This word describes the soft materials that are used to line a hamster's cage and nest box.

breed
A breed is a type of hamster. There are lots of different breeds of hamster – Syrian and Dwarf Russian are just two of them.

coat
An animal's fur is also known as its coat. Hamsters' coats can be long or short, and they come in many different colours.

grooming
When an animal's coat is gently brushed to remove any dust or dirt, it is called grooming.

hay
Hay is dried grass. It is full of goodness and keeps longer than fresh grass.

handling
Handling is when you pick up or touch a hamster. There is a special way to handle hamsters to keep them from getting hurt.

nest
Hamsters make nests where they feel safe and comfortable, for sleeping, eating or having babies.

pregnant
When a female hamster is pregnant, it means that she has got babies growing inside her.

pouch
Hamsters have a pouch in each cheek. The pouches are special pockets used for holding food and bedding.

rodent
Hamsters belong to the family of animals called rodents. Mice, rats and gerbils are also rodents.

solitary
A solitary animal is an animal that lives by itself most of the time. Adult Syrian hamsters are solitary animals.

veterinary surgeon
A veterinary surgeon, or vet, is an animal doctor. You should take a hamster to see a vet if it is ill or injured.

Find out more

Websites

www.pdsa.org.uk
Information on responsible pet care and how to join the PDSA's Pet Protectors club.

www.hamsters4kids.com
A website full of hamster information and cute photos.

www.hamsters-uk.org
The official website of the National Hamster Council.

www.rspca.org.uk
Go to the animal care page on hamsters for advice about caring for a hamster.

www.emmathevet.co.uk
You're bound to find the answers to questions about your hamster's health here.

Addresses

National Hamster Council
PO Box 154
Rotherham
South Yorkshire, S66 0FL

PDSA
Whitechapel Way
Priorslee
Telford
Shropshire
TF2 9PQ

I think I had better get surfing!

Index

B
babies 8, 28–29
bedding 5, 10, 11, 17, 19
biting 18, 19, 21
breeds 4, 6–7

C
cages 8, 10–11, 13, 16–17, 19, 20, 22, 23, 29
cats 10, 27
claws 24
coats 7, 29

D
dogs 27
dwarf hamsters 6, 7, 10, 26

E
ears 25
exercise 24, 26
exercise wheel 22

F
females 12, 26, 28
fighting 18, 26

food 5, 8, 10, 14–15, 16, 17, 21, 23, 29
fur 9, 24, 25

G
gerbils 27
grooming 25

H
handling 19, 20– 21
health 13, 24–25
hearts 4

M
males 12, 26
mice 4, 27
moods 18–19

N
nest boxes 11, 17
nests 29

P
paws 4, 5, 9, 24
pet shops 12, 14
pouches 5, 14

pregnancy 28–29
pups 28

R
rats 4, 27
rodents 4

S
senses 5
Syrian hamsters 4, 6, 7, 26

T
tails 4
teeth 5, 18, 21, 25
treats 15, 21
tunnels 10, 23

V
vets 24, 25

W
water 10, 15
wild hamsters 8–9, 10, 14, 23

Picture credits
t=top b=bottom m=middle l=left r=right

P & S Charmley: 7tr, 7ml, 7mt, 7mb, 7br, 26t, 29t, 29m; Warren Photographic: 8–9b, 27t, 26t, 28–29m